Dedication

For George – I love how your mind works and how you let your imagination expand every idea.

Copyright

© Copyright 2025 Deb Pickering. All Rights Reserved.

It is illegal to reproduce, duplicate or transmit any part of this document in either electronic means or printed format.

Recording of this publication is strictly prohibited

Nana Knows

George had been learning about the Victorians at school and seeing lots of black and white pictures. When he then sees his nana as a little girl, in black and white, he jumps to some very funny conclusions.

"Nana, when you were little, and the world was black and white,

Did you have to climb up chimneys, and have candles late at night?

Did you only have baths once a month, and did your dad go first?

So you bathed in dirty water? I bet that was the worst!

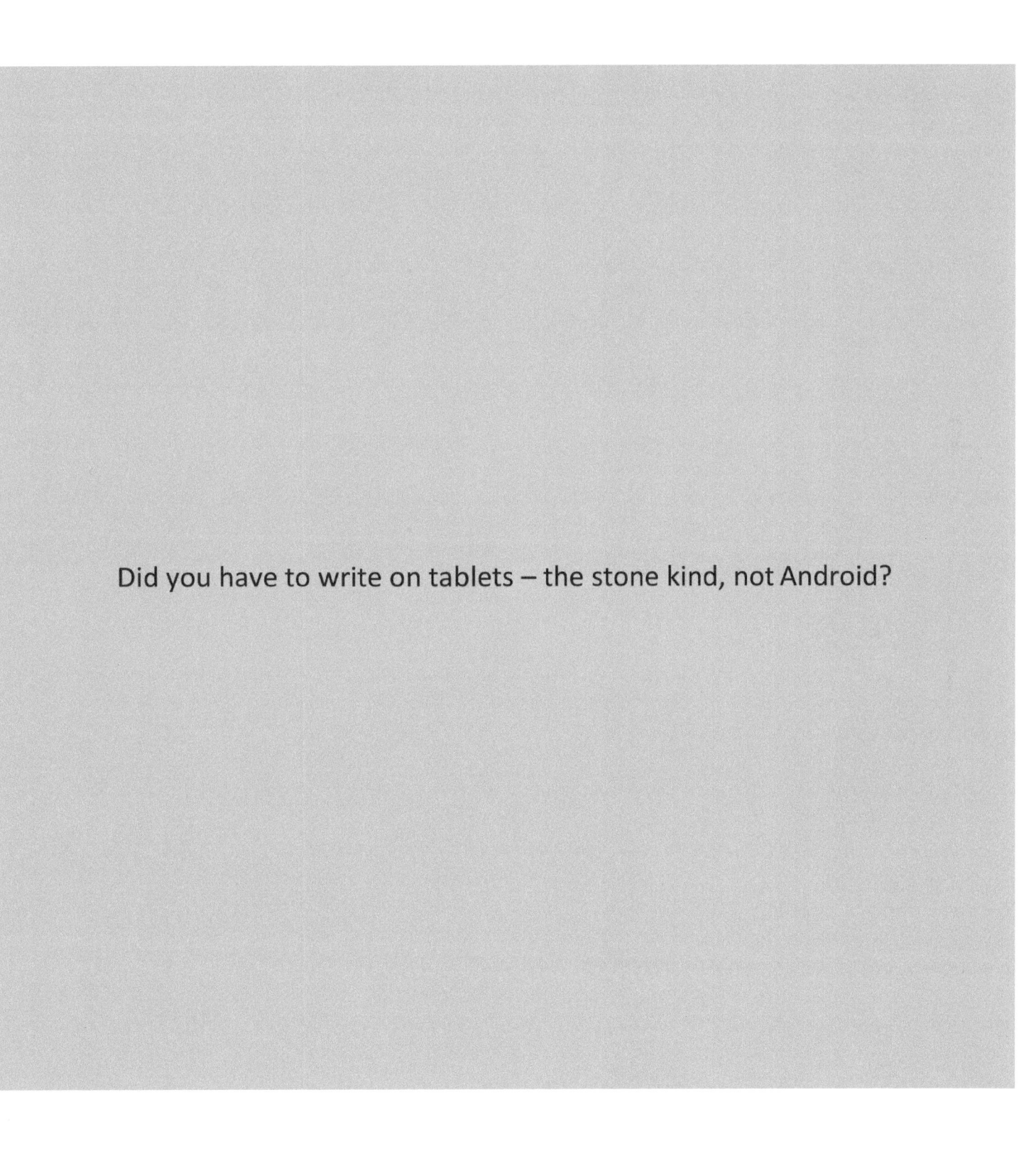

Did you have to write on tablets – the stone kind, not Android?

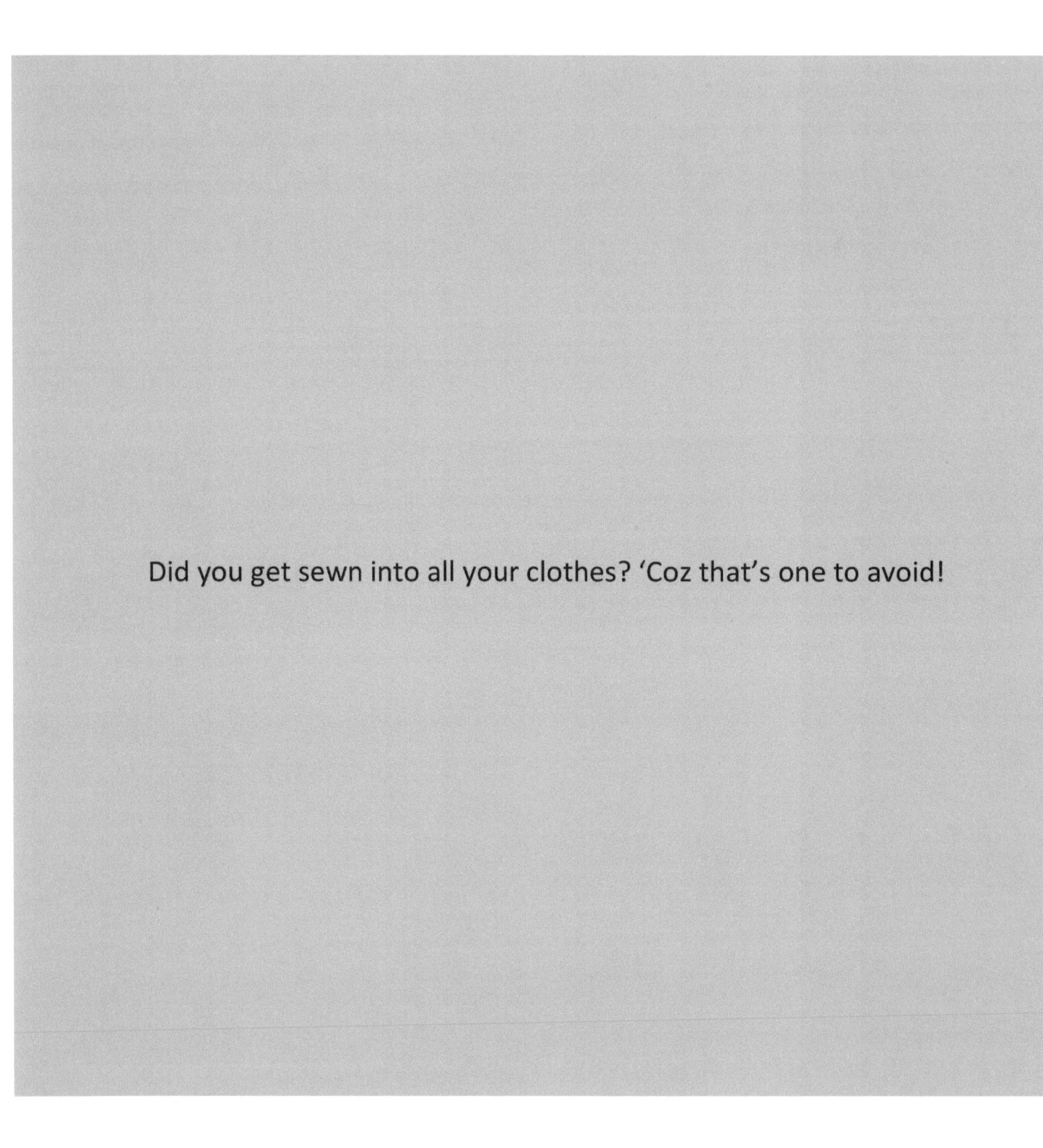

Did you get sewn into all your clothes? 'Coz that's one to avoid!

Did you have a pet dinosaur? I think I'd quite like that.

Unless it was something quite huge, that stood on you, and SPLAT!"

"I'm old, but I am not THAT old," said Nana with a grin.

"Where are you getting all this from?" She gently tweaked his chin.

"Well Grandad said to ask you; you're the oldest one I know.

He said that you know EVERYTHING!"

"Oh did he? Is that so?"

George nodded seriously. "Was he making a joke?"

"He was, because he thinks that he is such a funny bloke!"

"Go ask when his next show is, and can we still buy seats?

And then the oven's finished, and we'll eat our biscuit treats."

As George finished his biscuit, Nana leaned in and said.

"Please can you take the poop out, the pot's under the bed!"

Note to Parents: George had been learning about the Victorians: most children didn't go to school as you had to pay for schooling so they had to go to work from 4 or 5 years old, hence the question about climbing chimneys.

A poor family in Victorian times often would not have a bathroom, so would have a portable bath that was placed in front of the fire, in the kitchen, and filled with kettles of hot water. As this was so labour intensive, the whole family would take it in turns to use the same water and there would be a hierarchy, starting with the father.

It was around the 1700s that people often got sewn into their winter clothing in order to keep them warm and to stop draughts. The had a much different view on hygiene than we have today.

As indoor plumbing was rare, indoor toilets were also rare, so chamber pots were kept under the bed so that going to the toilet at night was easier. Obviously emptying it in the morning was no fun!

About the Author

Deb Pickering is a Nana of 3 gorgeous grandchildren, who lives in York with her husband. She loves being an active part of the children's lives and says, "They are an absolute inspiration, and better still, they make me laugh, which keeps me young!"